Quiet Time

BECOMING CONSISTENT IN YOUR DAILY DEVOTIONS

Time
for Busy
Women

6-WEEK DEVOTIONAL BY **ASHERITAH CIUCIU**

Cover & interior design by Flaviu Ciuciu

Proofreading by Vicki Caswell

Author photograph by Ashley McComb

For every woman who longs to be close to God
in the midst of the busyness:
may this book guide you into His presence.

Table of Contents

Scan this QR code
or go to **onethingalone.com/qtbw**
to get more devotionals and video tutorials.

Introduction

Welcome to Quiet Time for Busy Women!

This workbook is designed to help you become consistent in your daily devotions so you can experience deeper joy in your relationship with God.

I'm thrilled to embark on this journey with you. My prayer is that God will meet each of us where we are and take us deeper into His presence.

You'll find each week is structured as follows:

- A brief intro to that week's theme
- Daily devotions (Monday-Friday) prompts and space to respond
- Weekend space to reflect on what you learned and how you've grown

You'll also find the Quiet Time for Busy Women library referenced occasionally. It's available online at www.onethingalone.com/qtbw and includes helpful links, posts, and other resources to help you go deeper in your daily devotions.

Jesus doesn't promise to take away our busyness or to magically make our burdens disappear. But He promises something even better:

- Rest in the middle of busyness.
- Quiet in the eye of the storm.
- Joy in the midst of chaos.

We find all those things and more as we spend time in His presence.

Are you ready? Let's dig in.

Asheritah

Do anything, Lord,
that will fit me **to serve You**
and help my beloveds.

— Amy Carmichael

3 Simple Steps to Kick-Start Your Quiet Time

Like any goal worth achieving, becoming consistent in your Quiet Time habit doesn't happen by accident. You need to start with a plan and work that plan.

Here are three simple steps to set you up for success:

PICK YOUR GOAL

As you start, consider why you picked up this workbook. Many of us begin Bible-reading plans out of guilt or obligation, but those feelings aren't enough to keep us going when we face obstacles.

What is your goal for the next six weeks and why is it important to you? Write down your answers in a journal, and then ask God to help you experience victory.

PICK YOUR TIME

For many, mornings are the best time to find the quiet space they need to connect with God, but it's important to be realistic about your season of life. There's nothing inherently spiritual about being sleep-deprived just to fit daily devotions into your morning routine.

Pick a time that you can actually commit to keeping. Perhaps lunch time or evening works best for you. Or pick a habit that's already part of your daily routine (like eating breakfast, sitting in the carpool line, or brushing your teeth at night), and link your new Quiet Time habit to that established habit.

Try using this formula: "After I ___[insert established habit]___, I will sit down with my Bible and this workbook for my Quiet Time." The point isn't to come to God "the right way" but with a right heart.

PICK YOUR REWARD

Recent research into habit formation reveals that we're more likely to stick with habits when they're enjoyable to do and when we look forward to a reward at the end. Our greatest reward will always be growing in our knowledge and love of Jesus, and as we celebrate this, we'll reinforce a positive feedback loop in our brains that will make us look forward to our Quiet Time with excitement.

But we can also journal what we're learning, use a daily habit tracker (Type-A sisters, rejoice!), do a happy dance, text a friend, or reward ourselves with something that reinforces our Quiet Time habit (like Bible highlighters, a journaling Bible, a Scripture mug, or tickets to a Christian concert or conference).

Have fun with this! After all, God created us to enjoy Him and to be enjoyed by Him. He's not giving out brownie points for the most boring Quiet Time. Of course, there will be days when we show up to our Bibles out of sheer obedience even when we don't feel like it, but on those days, we can ask God to fills us with desire for Him and with joy in His presence, and He will! (See Psalm 16:11)

Remember, the goal isn't perfection—it's progress. God is more interested in our growth over time than in a short-lived streak. Consider the next six weeks your springboard into a lifetime habit of seeking God daily. Ask God to help you develop both the will and the way to grow closer to Him, and watch as He answers. God delights in revealing Himself to us as we seek Him with all our hearts.

May you discover the joy of God's presence as you draw near to Him each day. And may your life be changed forever.

Monday

Read Psalm 92:1-2. Write it out in the space below.

According to this psalm, when is a good time to praise God?

List below the different ways the psalmist says we can connect with God.

If you haven't already, decide on your goal, time, and reward for Quiet Time. Write down your plan in the space below. Then rewrite it on a post-it note and place it somewhere you'll see it so you don't forget.

Spend a few minutes praising God for being available 24/7. Write down specific ways He has shown love and faithfulness to you, and worship Him with gladness.

Tuesday

Read John 6:44 and Romans 8:26-27. Write out one of the passages in the space below.

What do these passages say about God's role in our relationship with Him?

We cannot seek God on our own; we need Him to draw us to Himself – and He faithfully does that and more, interceding on our behalf when we don't even know how to move forward. How does this reality affect your relationship with God?

Today, confess your desperate need for God. In the space below, ask Him to draw your heart nearer to His and to give you a burning desire for Him.

Wednesday

Read Isaiah 30:15. Write out the verse in the space below.

Oftentimes our "quiet time" is anything but quiet. We pray, we read, we write, and we sing. But when was the last time you were actually quiet before God?

Today, practice resting before the Lord. Set a 5-minute timer if you like, or just allow yourself to take a few minutes to quiet your body, mind, and heart. Exchange your worry for His peace; your striving for His sovereignty; and your tiredness for His energy. If any distracting thoughts come to mind, write them on a sticky note or in the space below and return to your quiet rest.

In our fast-paced world, it can be very difficult to quiet our minds. What did you learn about yourself, about God, and about worship during your five minutes of quiet?

Thursday

Read Philippians 2:13. Write it out below.

This passage states that God gives us both the desire and the ability to do His good will, including being consistent in meeting with Him. What does this say about God?

Of the two, which do you need help with most: the desire for Quiet Time or the ability to be consistent in your Quiet Time?

Write a brief prayer asking God to work in you the desire and ability to be consistent in your relationship with Him. End by expressing your trust that He will be faithful to His promise, and praise Him for His trustworthiness.

Friday

Read Revelation 4:1-11. Pick one of the verses and write it below.

How does this text describe the ongoing reality of God's throne room? What is happening there right now?

How does your personal Quiet Time contribute to or reflect the worship happening in heaven?

Draw a picture or diagram below to show how your individual Quiet Time and the heavenly worship combine to bring a pleasant offering to God.

Weekend Reflection

What did you learn about God this week?

What did you learn about yourself this week?

What did you learn about Quiet Time this week?

Write an honest prayer to God, responding to what you've learned.

Notes

_____

_____

_____

_____

_____

_____

_____

_____

_____

_____

_____

_____

_____

_____

_____

_____

_____

_____

_____

_____

Notes

_____

_____

_____

_____

_____

_____

_____

_____

_____

_____

_____

_____

_____

_____

_____

_____

_____

_____

_____

_____

Notes

_____
_____
_____
_____
_____
_____
_____
_____
_____
_____
_____
_____
_____
_____
_____
_____
_____
_____
_____
_____
_____

Notes

_____

_____

_____

_____

_____

_____

_____

_____

_____

_____

_____

_____

_____

_____

_____

_____

_____

_____

_____

_____

_____

Every one of us is as
close to God
as he has chosen to be.

– J. Oswald Sanders

The Critical Step that 92% of People Forget

How many times have you started a new habit, only to fail?

Chances are the answer is "lots of times."

According to the Journal of Clinical Psychology, only 8% of people successfully achieve their resolutions. That means the rest of us start, stumble, and just give up.

But here's the critical step that's keeping us from success: we must treat failure as our friend and learn from our mistakes.

If you've ever started a Bible-reading plan and given up, you know how discouraging that can feel. But have you ever taken time to think about why you quit? What obstacles stood in your way? What struggles did you face? What frustrations kept you from pushing forward?

In order to make Quiet Time a consistent habit, you must learn from your past mistakes and anticipate obstacles that may come up. Then, brainstorm creative ways to overcome those obstacles and persevere in your discipline.

Here are a few examples of what commonly derails us, and how we can get back on track:

SOCIAL MEDIA

Perhaps you're skipping Quiet Time because you get sucked in by your phone or computer. That happens to many of us. Acknowledge that social media can keep you from seeking Quiet Time with God, and then determine to not get online until you've first met with God.

SLEEPING IN

If sleeping in past your alarm clock is a struggle, make it a priority to go to bed earlier. Put your alarm on the other side of the room. Or consider picking another time for your daily appointment with God.

SCHEDULE DEVIATIONS

Whether it's kids waking up early or everyone sleeping in on a holiday, a schedule deviation can throw us off our game. For early risers, put together an activity basket to keep them busy, or include family members in your Quiet Time, modeling for them how you meet with God.

FALLING BEHIND

If you've missed a few days, it's easy to feel discouraged and overwhelmed. But instead of trying to catch up, give yourself permission to skip those readings and pick up with the current day's reading. You can always go back and read the days you've missed another time.

Anyone who starts a new habit will encounter friction and resistance. You're not a failure just because you've missed a day. Or two. Or ten. It takes time to establish a new habit. So rather than viewing obstacles as signs that we should just give up, let's begin to view them as opportunities to think creatively and develop perseverance.

Our reward isn't just belonging to the 8% few who succeed, though that may be true; our reward is deeper intimacy with Jesus. And that's worth every effort.

Monday

Read Lamentations 3:22-23. Write it out below.

Regardless of how much we've "failed" at spending Quiet Time with God in the past, God still welcomes us into a new adventure with Him. What does this passage say about His love and compassion?

How does this daily renewal affect God's disposition toward you?

Write a prayer of adoration, praise, and worship for how God loves you.

Tuesday

Read Psalm 51:1-19. Pick one verse that stands out to you and write it below.

What obstacles to consistent Quiet Time have you faced in the past?

In what ways have you chosen other pursuits before God?

When King David wrote this psalm, he was grieving over his sins. Using his prayer as a guide, confess your sins, naming them specifically.

Now read 1 John 1:8-9 and write it below, personalizing it using your name. Receive God's forgiveness, and praise Him for His faithfulness in the lines below.

Wednesday

Read Matthew 11:28-30. Write the passage in the space provided.

Faced with our shortcomings, we often want to try harder to do what's right. But what does Jesus invite us to do in today's passage?

How does the concept of "rest for your soul" relate to spending time with Jesus?

Write a prayer to God, expressing your response to Jesus' invitation, and then spend 5 minutes in quiet stillness before the Lord, receiving His rest.

Write down any thoughts or impressions from your time of stillness:

Thursday

Read Isaiah 43:18-19 and write it out below.

This week we've spent a lot of time talking about past failures and obstacles. What does today's passage say about the past, the present, and the future?

How would your Quiet Time habit change if you believed God's promise in this text?

Write down this passage on an index card and post it on your mirror, on your fridge, in your car, or somewhere else you will see it daily to remind you that God is doing a new thing in your life.

Friday

Read Hebrews 4:14-16 and write it out below. Then underline the words that refer to God and circle the words that describe how we should act in light of God's character.

In the Old Testament, a High Priest had the role of intervening on behalf of the people before a holy and righteous God to secure His forgiveness. What kind of a High Priest does this passage say Jesus is? How does that affect us?

In the space below, list the obstacles that have kept you from consistent Quiet Time. Next to each obstacle, write down a specific way you could overcome that obstacle the next time you come up against it.

Picture yourself kneeling before the throne of God, and lay your list at His feet. Confident that Jesus empathizes with our weaknesses, ask Him for mercy, grace, and strength to overcome these obstacles and experience victory in the days and weeks to come.

Weekend Reflection

What did you learn about God this week?

What did you learn about yourself this week?

What did you learn about Quiet Time this week?

Write an honest prayer to God, responding to what you've learned.

Notes

Notes

Notes

Notes

_____

_____

_____

_____

_____

_____

_____

_____

_____

_____

_____

_____

_____

_____

_____

_____

_____

_____

_____

_____

_____

_____

_____

We must exchange **whispers** with God before **shouts** with the world.

– Lysa TerKeurst

Discovering Your Best Way to Do Quiet Time

Are you a visual, kinesthetic, or auditory learner?

What about personality type: are you an introvert or extrovert? Thinker or feeler?

How about chocolate: milk, white, or dark?

I'm just kidding about that last question (though I'm finally acquiring a taste for dark chocolate). But those other questions are legitimate, and you probably answered them in your mind without giving it much thought.

The truth is we intuitively know how we function best when it comes to learning, relating to people, and consuming content, and we adjust our approach based on what works best for us. But when it comes to the spiritual realm, we somehow expect everyone to relate to God in the same way. After all, doesn't God expect us to read the Bible in solitude and wrap it up with a tidy prayer?

Turns out, God's more creative than we think. Throughout history, He's invited people to connect with Him in myriad ways, before the Bible was even available in individual printed copies.

- How do you think Enoch walked with God?

- How did David have his "Quiet Time" in the pastures when he was a shepherd boy?

- How did Mary keep her heart in tune with God?

- What about all the Christians who lived throughout the Middle Ages and those who couldn't read?

I'm not saying that reading the Bible and praying are optional for spiritual development. I believe they are essential, and we are privileged to live in an era when we have the Word of God readily available to us. But let's not believe the lie that there's only one "right" way to connect with God.

In fact, as we look at Scripture, we discover that God delights in diversity, artistry, and creativity. And just as a parent delights in watching their children grow into their unique talents and personalities, so I believe God delights in watching us bloom into the spiritual people He created us to be.

Some of us feel closest to God while hiking a mountain or watching the fiery colors of a sunrise. Others feel a deep connection with God through reciting ancient creeds and participating in traditions. Still others feel His presence when serving a meal to the homeless or caring for an elderly parent.

It's time we unboxed our perception of what it means to connect with God and embrace the freedom, creativity, and beauty of connecting with Him in the ways He's created us to. As we learn our spiritual temperament, we will discover the freedom of not just dutifully "doing" our Quiet Time, but actually enjoying fullness of joy in God's presence.

Monday

Read Psalm 150. List below all the ways we are instructed to praise the Lord.

How are all the praise methods similar? How is each one different from the others?

What does this diversity say about God and how He receives praise?

Write a prayer thanking God for creating variety and artistry and providing us with different skills to all combine together in a wonderful symphony of worship. Thank Him specifically for the ways He has created you and gifted you to praise Him.

Tuesday

Read James 1:5 and write it out below.

In reflecting on yesterday's assignment, which of the praise methods listed are you most comfortable with? Why?

Which of the praise methods listed yesterday make you uncomfortable? Why?

If our entire lives we've thought there's only one way to connect with God, we probably need help discovering the depths of who God created us to be. What does today's verse say about God's response to our need for wisdom?

Today, ask God to open your eyes and your mind, to give you wisdom to understand the ways He's created to worship Him, connect with Him, and serve Him. Then take the Creative Devotions Quiz available in the Quiet Time for Busy Women library (www.onethingalone.com/qtbw) to discover how you naturally draw near to God.

Wednesday

Read Psalm 23:1-3 and write it out below. Underline the ways the Shepherd cares for His sheep.

What is the sheep's responsibility in this passage?

What does this picture reveal about our relationship with God?

How can you practice trusting, following, and resting in God today?

Take 5 minutes to be still in His presence, letting the Good Shepherd lead you into green pastures and by still waters. Afterwards, write down any thoughts or impressions that come to mind.

Thursday

Read Jeremiah 29:12-14 and write it out below. Then underline God's actions and circle our actions.

What does God promise to His people in this passage?

In what ways can you seek God with your whole heart?

Write a short prayer in your journal in response to God's promise.

Friday

Read 1 Corinthians 10:31 and write it in the space below.

What does this text say about how we can glorify God?

Have you been trying to fit into someone else's picture of what an "ideal Quiet Time" looks like?

How have the readings this week affected your perspective?

At some point today, read 120 Creative Ways to Connect with God (available at www.onethingalone.com/qtbw) to discover creative methods to connect with God. Then choose an activity you haven't done before and schedule a time to do it this weekend.

Weekend Reflection

What did you learn about God this week?

What did you learn about yourself this week?

What did you learn about Quiet Time this week?

Write an honest prayer to God, responding to what you've learned.

Notes

_____

_____

_____

_____

_____

_____

_____

_____

_____

_____

_____

_____

_____

_____

_____

_____

_____

_____

_____

_____

_____

Notes

_____

_____

_____

_____

_____

_____

_____

_____

_____

_____

_____

_____

_____

_____

_____

_____

_____

_____

_____

_____

_____

_____

Notes

_____

_____

_____

_____

_____

_____

_____

_____

_____

_____

_____

_____

_____

_____

_____

_____

_____

_____

_____

_____

_____

_____

_____

_____

Notes

Try not to think of the time you spend with God as a duty. The purpose of a quiet time is for you to get to **know God**. And as you come to know Him, you can walk out of your special times with God enjoying a living relationship with Him that you can cultivate all day long — throughout all your life.

– Henry Blackaby

How Little Changes Become Big Transformations

My toddler is recently obsessed with ice cubes. Whenever my back is turned, he grabs a few ice cubes out of the freezer and runs off to play, meaning I find puddles where I least expect them.

But have you ever watched ice melt? It's agonizingly slow.

Imagine you're a scientist. You set a cube of ice on a plate and grab your notebook and pen, ready to mark your observations. If the temperature in the room is 15 degrees Fahrenheit, nothing's going to happen to the ice. It remains frozen. So what happens if you turn up the thermostat to 16 degrees? Nothing. Of course.

17 degrees? Still nothing.

Even though real change is happening in the atmosphere, the ice remains frozen. How frustrating! But finally, after lots of tiny changes, you turn the knob to 32 degrees and to your delight—the ice begins to melt! You notice that the higher you turn the thermostat, the faster the ice melts until you're finally left with a little puddle.

Question: Which degree change was most important? Answer: Each of them.

You might have thought that the change from 31 to 32 was most important, but truthfully, they're each important because if you would have given up the experiment at 26 degrees or even at 31 degrees, you'd never have reached the melting point.

Each tiny change led to the next until you finally saw your desired result. But it's easy to give up in the waiting, isn't it? We want instant results, but radical transformation happens little by little on this journey with Jesus, one day at a time. God calls us to "a long obedience in the same direction," as Eugene Peterson would say, and most days may seem rather boring as we do the same thing over and over again, with very little noticeable change. But make no mistake, friend—God is at work.

In our lifelong Quiet Time journey:

- Sometimes, we'll do our devotions but not feel euphoric in God's presence.

- Sometimes, we'll pray hard without seeing results.

- Sometimes, we'll go for days or weeks without consistent time with God.

- Sometimes, we'll wonder if it's worth saying "no" to the flesh and "yes" to the Spirit.

Don't be discouraged, friend. God is at work.

We may not be able to pinpoint the exact moment that our hearts begin to long for time in God's Word, or that talking to God on our commute becomes second nature, but over time God's warm love begins to thaw our hearts as we spend time in His presence until we're transformed beyond recognition. Little by little adds up.

- Over time, you WILL see progress if you don't give up.

- God promises that He WILL reward those who diligently seek Him.

- Your ceaseless prayers WILL be answered in due time.

- Studying the Bible WILL result in a deeper knowledge and love for God.

- Surrendering to the Spirit's leading WILL lead to increased Christlikeness.

Trust that God is faithful, and He will graciously use your faithfulness in the little things to lead you to a greater transformation into the image of Jesus Himself.

Monday

Read Psalm 27:1-14. Write down two or three verses that resonate with you.

Why did you pick those verses?

This psalm describes David's quiet hope in God's deliverance even when surrounded by the enemy. How can you relate your "in between" feelings to David's?

Write a prayer praising God for His faithfulness and steadfastness in your times of waiting.

Tuesday

Read John 15:1-9. Using the space below, summarize this passage in your own words.

What does Jesus say is necessary in order to bear fruit?

How does the picture of the vine and the branches help you visualize the importance of remaining connected to Jesus?

Sometimes we need to remind ourselves just how dependent we are on God, especially if we're self-motivated and self-reliant in other areas of our lives. Today, spend time expressing your neediness to God. Write a prayer confessing any area of your life where you've tried to achieve change on your own, and ask Him to help you stay connected to Him.

Wednesday

Read Psalm 46:10 and write it out in the space below.

How does the knowledge that God is sovereign help us be still?

Write down the top 3-5 things that are heavy on your heart.

One by one, give the things you listed to God, and then be still. Rest in His power and might to handle those situations. If thoughts come to mind, tell them to the Lord, and then be quiet again. Receive His rest, and allow His presence to soothe your weary soul. If you'd like, write down any thoughts or impressions you had during your time of stillness.

Thursday

Read Philippians 1:6 and write it out below.

What does this passage say about who begins work in us? What about who ends it?

If we surrender to God, whose responsibility is our continued growth? How can this truth free you from discouragement and hopelessness when you don't see progress?

Think back to where you were a month ago, a year ago, or ten years ago. Do you see growth? In what ways?

Write a prayer of praise to God for what He has done in your life, and express your trust in Him to continue working, even in the seasons of faithful waiting.

Friday

Read Psalm 9:1, 11 and write the verses below.

What does David say he will do in verse 1?

What does he charge the people to do in verse 11?

In the space below, write down 3-5 specific blessings in your life right now.

If you haven't already, keep a running list of God's specific blessings in your life. Watch how this list grows, and read it when you're discouraged. Also consider keeping a record of your specific prayer requests, as well as the date and way in which God answered. These records of God's faithfulness will encourage you to keep persevering when times are tough. And when you feel like you have nothing to praise God for, they will remind your heart of all the reasons you have to praise Him.

Weekend Reflection

What did you learn about God this week?

What did you learn about yourself this week?

What did you learn about Quiet Time this week?

Write an honest prayer to God, responding to what you've learned.

Notes

Notes

Notes

_____

_____

_____

_____

_____

_____

_____

_____

_____

_____

_____

_____

_____

_____

_____

_____

_____

_____

_____

Notes

_____

_____

_____

_____

_____

_____

_____

_____

_____

_____

_____

_____

_____

_____

_____

_____

_____

_____

_____

_____

_____

_____

The nearer we **come to God**, the more graciously will He reveal himself to us.

– *C. H. Spurgeon*

What's the Big Deal about Quiet Time Anyway?

Last week we talked about the melting ice cube.

Changing habits, especially ingrained ones that we've practiced for years, is hard. We need to tap into the deeper motivation that will help us choose discipline over comfort.

To become consistent in time with God, we need to understand why we should spend time with God and how that will impact our lives if we want to overcome those obstacles we talked about in Week 2.

So ask yourself: Why do you want to be consistent in your Quiet Time with God?

- Do you feel guilty?

- Think it's expected of you?

- Want to impress God with your obedience?

- Trying to reassure God He chose well when He adopted you as a child?

- Want to set an example for your husband or children?

I could put a checkmark next to each one of those reasons, and plenty more; but they won't keep us motivated in the long run, because they all miss the point.

God doesn't want us to spend time with Him to fulfill a duty or make Him feel better. God wants us to spend time with Him because in His presence we discover fullness of joy and we become transformed into the very people He created us to be.

Being consistent in our Quiet Time helps us

- discover life as God meant us to live,

- experience the depths of intimacy with Him,

- grow in our love and knowledge of Him, and

- walk in step with His Spirit inside us.

In other words, the reason God wants us to be consistent in our Quiet Time is to find more joy and satisfaction in life with Him. If our motivation is anything less than that, we will soon abandon our good intentions and lapse back into complacency. As John Piper says, "God is most glorified in us when we are most satisfied in Him." His glory and our enjoyment of Him are intertwined.

David says, "Earnestly I seek you. My soul thirsts for you" (Psalm 63:1). And later "Because your love is better than life, my lips will praise you" (Psalm 63:3). And elsewhere: "In your presence is fullness of joy. At your right hand are pleasures forevermore" (Psalm 16:11). What David writes about isn't a stale exercise in religion; it's the rich, abundant, satisfying reality of God's own presence.

If this sounds too good to be true, I encourage you to talk to God about it. Ask Him if it's possible to experience this kind of joy, intimacy, and purpose in life. And He will gladly and tenderly show you the fullness of joy found at the feet of Jesus today and every day.

Monday

Read Psalm 16:11 and write it below.

What does David say God does for him?

What does this say about God's character and His attitude toward His children?

Have you experienced what David describes here in this passage? If yes, when and where? If no, why not?

Write a prayer expressing praise, thanks, and adoration for God's faithfulness, His goodness, and the ways He has personally shown you love in your life.

Tuesday

Read Psalm 63:1-8. Write out the verse that most resonates with you below.

How does David describe his feelings toward God?

Could you honestly say the same things are true of your life? Why or why not?

Open your heart toward God, and tell Him how you really feel about Him. If you're bored with your Quiet Time, tell Him. If you're angry with God, tell Him. If you're in a slump, tell Him. (Be honest with the Lord. He knows your heart already.)

Ask God to begin stirring in you a hunger and a longing for Him. Even our desire for God comes from Him, so if you don't have that desire, ask Him for it.

Wednesday

Read Psalm 131:1-3. Write verse 2 below.

How does David describe his soul in the presence of God in verse 2?

How does a weaned child differ from a nursing child in his or her mother's arms? What does the child want from the mother in each case?

How does this picture help you visualize finding stillness in God's presence?

Picture yourself as a little child, climbing up in God's lap, putting your head on His shoulder, and just listening to His heart. Rest there. Let go of all expectations, wants, or longings. Spend a few minutes just enjoying His embrace and let His presence quiet your soul within you. Afterwards, write your thoughts below.

Thursday

Read Hebrews 11:6 and James 4:8. Write one of the passages below.

What do these passages say about God's response to those who seek Him?

What do they imply are our responsibilities in our relationship with God?

Do you believe God wants you to enjoy Him? Why or why not?

What kinds of "rewards" have you sought from your Quiet Time in the past?

Based on the passages you've studied this week, what kinds of rewards can you expect from spending time with God?

Friday

Read Psalm 118:14-16. Write verse 15 in the space provided below.

What's the tone of this passage? In other words, what are the primary emotions expressed here?

What does this passage say the righteous do?

What kinds of "mighty things" have you seen God do in your own life today? This last week? This past month?

Today, turn your Quiet Time into a time of joyful celebration. Allow God's power and might to lift your spirit as you praise Him for what He's done for you personally and in the lives of those around you. Have fun with this—turn it into a party! Think confetti, cupcakes, dancing, singing, fist pumping, and hollering for joy. God enjoys a good party even more than we do. Let His presence fill you with joy, and may your worship bring a smile to His face as well.

Weekend Reflection

What did you learn about God this week?

What did you learn about yourself this week?

What did you learn about Quiet Time this week?

Write an honest prayer to God, responding to what you've learned.

Notes

Notes

Notes

_____

_____

_____

_____

_____

_____

_____

_____

_____

_____

_____

_____

_____

_____

_____

_____

_____

_____

_____

_____

_____

Notes

_____

_____

_____

_____

_____

_____

_____

_____

_____

_____

_____

_____

_____

_____

_____

_____

_____

_____

_____

_____

_____

_____

You move us to delight in
praising You, because **You have
made us for Yourself**,
and our hearts are restless
until they can find peace in You.

– St. Augustine

Three Little Words that Will Change Your Life

I would love to grab coffee with you.

If I could, I'd sit across from you with a mocha and listen to your story. I'd ask about where you grew up, when you first learned about God's love for you, and how He gradually drew you into His presence. I'd listen to the ways He's sustained you through heartbreak, and I'd celebrate with you His mighty victories.

But I also know I'd hear stories that go like this: "I was born and raised in a Christian family. I said the sinner's prayer in grade school, and I've been trying to be a good Christian ever since. But God isn't interested in my life. Nothing exciting has every happened to me."

Sound familiar? Ever heard someone say that? Have you said that yourself?

We all long to live lives of significance. We read of Mother Teresa, Jim Elliot, Amy Carmichael, D. L. Moody, and secretly whisper, "I wish I could change the world." But then we go back to the casserole dishes and loads of laundry, the office politics and quarterly reports, and figure God's just not interested in little ol' us.

But nothing could be further from the truth.

Right now, this very second, God is searching the earth for women and men to use in great Kingdom work. And He's not looking for the best-educated or most-qualified. Nope. He's looking for just one quality: surrender.

Think of the people God used at critical junctures in Israel's history:

- Moses was a criminal hiding in the desert. But God used him to lead the captive Israelites out of Egypt and teach them His laws.

- Samuel was a servant boy despised by the priest's sons, but God used him to guide the nation into the turbulent era of kingship.

- Isaiah was a man terrorized by the Assyrians but God used him to proclaim His salvation through the coming Messiah.

- Mary was a teenage girl in a backwater town, but God used her to bring His Son into the world and raise Him as her own.

What do these four history-makers have in common? Well, other than the fact that they were seriously under-qualified for the job, they all said these three little words: "Here I am."

God doesn't need your degrees or your qualifications. He isn't impressed with your daily devotions, Bible studies or community service projects. God is looking for women and men who are so enraptured by His love and grace that they surrender their lives to Him and say, "Here I am. All I have is Yours. Do with me whatever You want."

If you feel your testimony isn't that impressive, I invite you to make these three little words your daily prayer: "Here I am." Then watch as God takes your life and transforms it into a world-changing, history-shifting, eternity-pointing narrative, so that everyone who hears it says, "Whoa! Look what God did there. I want Him to do that in my life, too!" Because He can. And He will.

And that's quite the story to share over coffee.

Monday

Read 2 Chronicles 16:7-9. Summarize the first sentence in verse 9 in your own words below.

What does this passage say God did for the king in the past and how did the king respond?

Who does it say God is searching for?

Do you believe God actually wants to use you in world-changing ways? Why or why not?

Write a prayer praising God for the ways that He uses insignificant people to do great things, and surrender your life to Him, praying "Here I am."

Tuesday

Read Luke 1:26-38. Pick a verse that stands out to you and write it below.

This is a well-known passage about Mary, but look specifically at her reactions. How does she first respond to the angel? What emotions are evident in the text?

How would you have reacted to the angel's news?

There were lots of unknowns for Mary, and many reasons to be afraid. In your own life, what fears hold you back from complete surrender?

What are you afraid God will ask you to do if you give Him complete control? Write out a prayer confessing these things to the Lord, and pray, "Here I am."

Wednesday

Read 1 Peter 5:6 and write it in the space below.

What are we told to do in this verse?

What does that look like in your daily life?

What does this passage say about God's timing?

Why is it hard to wait for God to act?

Today, spend five minutes being still in God's presence, and tell Him, "Here I am."

Thursday

Read Luke 9:23-24 and write out the verses below.

What does Jesus say it means to follow Him?

Have you given God complete control of your life?

Although a life of surrender begins with a specific decision to give God control, it is also a daily practice, requiring that we submit to God every day. What keeps you from daily surrender?

Write a prayer confessing the things that hold you back from complete surrender, and then say, "Here I am."

Friday

Read Romans 12:1-2 and write it in the space below.

In the Old Testament, people often built altars on which they sacrificed offerings in order to remember significant moments with God. What does this passage say is our offering to God?

As you begin to live a life surrendered to God, what's a symbolic "altar" you can build to remember this commitment? It may be a photo, a framed verse, or a smooth stone from your garden. Think creatively about this, and then place it somewhere prominent so you are reminded of your commitment to surrender to God every time you see it. Then pray, "Here I am."

Weekend Reflection

What did you learn about God this week?

What did you learn about yourself this week?

What did you learn about Quiet Time this week?

Write an honest prayer to God, responding to what you've learned.

Notes

_____
_____
_____
_____
_____
_____
_____
_____
_____
_____
_____
_____
_____
_____
_____
_____
_____
_____
_____
_____
_____

Notes

Notes

_____

_____

_____

_____

_____

_____

_____

_____

_____

_____

_____

_____

_____

_____

_____

_____

_____

_____

_____

_____

_____

Notes

_____

_____

_____

_____

_____

_____

_____

_____

_____

_____

_____

_____

_____

_____

_____

_____

_____

_____

_____

_____

_____

_____

The world has yet to see
what God can do
with a man [or woman]
fully consecrated to Him.

– D. L. Moody

You're Finished! Now What?

You did it! You completed the Quiet Time for Busy Women six-week journey. I hope these weeks helped you grow deeper in your relationship with God as well as establish a daily devotions habit.

Now that you're finished, you may be wondering, "What's next?"

I'm glad you're asking that, because it's an important next step in your journey. A surprising number of people who run a marathon, stop running altogether in the weeks that follow, losing all the endurance they've worked so hard to achieve during training. The same is true for many of us who complete a Bible-reading plan.

Don't let the finish line lure you back into complacency. Instead, use it to propel you on to bigger and greater things.

Here are a few ideas of what you could do next:

- Get my devotional Walking with God and go deeper in your Quiet Time habit (link available in the Quiet Time for Busy Women resource library at www.onethingalone.com/qtbw).

- Invite a few girlfriends to go through this study together

- Join a Bible study in your local church that includes daily readings of Scripture

- Sign up for an online community Bible study

Whatever you choose to do next, DO SOMETHING!

Use what you learned in these six weeks to launch you into a lifetime of growing intimacy with God. Feel free to revisit the lessons when you need a refresher:

Week 1: Make a plan that works for you and then work the plan.

Week 2: Reflect on what works and make tweaks to enjoy your Quiet Time more.

Week 3: Include creative and fun worship days that suit your spiritual temperament.

Week 4: Keep persevering even when you don't see results right away.

Week 5: Periodically check your motivation and ask God to increase your joy in Him.

Week 6: Surrender your life to God every day and watch Him do great things.

If you've enjoyed this book, please leave a review on Amazon and tell someone about it. (Think girlfriends, moms, aunts, small-group friends, coworkers, and even hairstylists.) Your recommendation will help more women become consistent in their daily devotions and discover the joy of God's presence.

It's been such a pleasure leading you through these last six weeks. I hope to "see" you in another study soon!

With much joy,

Asheritah

About the Author

Asheritah Ciuciu is a bestselling writer and speaker, wife to her high school sweetheart Flaviu and mama to three spunky kiddos. She grew up in Romania as a missionary kid and studied English and Women's Ministry at Cedarville University. Her passion is helping overwhelmed women find joy in Jesus through creative and consistent time in God's Word. Download your free guide to Cultivate Consistent Quiet Time with Jesus at www.OneThingAlone.com.

Scan this QR code
or go to **onethingalone.com/qtbw**
to get more devotionals and video tutorials.

Made in the USA
Coppell, TX
16 January 2024

27732073R10077